PIONEERS OF BASEBALL

RUSS COHEN

MOtivational PRESS®
LEADERS IN GLOBAL PUBLISHING

Published by Motivational Press, Inc.
1777 Aurora Road
Melbourne, Florida, 32935
www.MotivationalPress.com

Manufactured in the United States of America.

ISBN: 978-1-62865-446-2

CONTENTS

ACKNOWLEDGMENTS

Thanks to Motivational Press for making this project possible.

Thanks to Clark Groome, for providing great support
and old time baseball knowledge that's hard to find.

Thanks to Pete Weber who took a great interest in this book sight unseen!

Thanks to Mike Augello for your help and support.

Thanks to my family and friends for always being supportive.

Thanks to the New York Public Library who digitized this great collection.

Thanks to those who have kept this great game alive.

Baseball is a perfect game. The long season coincides with warm weather and good times. "Opening Day" is still my favorite event to attend. It's a day filled with optimism and hope.

Russ Cohen

ALBERT SPALDING

This book explores the early teams of the National and American League such as the Philadelphia Quakers, who were founded in 1883, later changed their name to the Philadelphias and became the Phillies in 1890.

It also takes a look at the stars of that period, like pitcher/outfielder Dan Casey, pitcher/outfielder/ first baseman Charlie Buffington, infielder Napoleon "Nap" Lajoie and third baseman/shortstop Hans Lobert, who once raced a quarter horse around a baseball diamond.

The formative years of baseball had a number of characters, including Albert Spalding. Spalding was one of the early pioneers and driving forces in the game, who helped form the National League after retiring at the age of 27. He also made sure that the new league used Spalding baseballs, which were sold exclusively at his sporting goods stores.

Brooklyn is loaded with trendy restaurants and baseball history. In 1859, a sportswriter Henry Chadwick invented the box score. Years later, the Brooklyn Bridegrooms joined the National League.

The rules of the game were very different back then. The game was still evolving. There was a big change from 1870 to 1871. The dimensions of the baseball were outlined (not less than five nor more than five and one-quarter ounces, same as today).

It had to be composed of India rubber and yarn and covered with leather. The rubber was exactly one ounce. Some have suspected that's been experimented with over the years. The modern-day baseball has a cushioned cork center, surrounded by black rubber and another layer of red rubber.

The bat has to be made of wood and no other material is acceptable. Cane was used as it is a species of wood and Bamboo as well, along with maple, hickory in today's game.

A walk was three balls, the strike zone was knee to shoulders and pitchers could no longer balk or fake a delivery. That was a game changer, as an unfair delivery could have meant a forfeiture of the game if the umpire was so inclined.

Batting out of order was addressed. Once the lineup was set in the first inning that was the lineup.

A change to the rules gave the umpire the option to call a runner out who had been tagged out with the ball in the hand of the fielder but then dropped based on collision.

In 1872, the 9-inning format was the rule. In 1873, a ball caught on a fly or a bounce (fair or foul) was an out. Before 1930, a baseball that bounced over a fence was a home run.

There was no moonlighting. Members of the association couldn't play in a "match" game for extra money.

Spalding started playing in 1871 and turned out to be a huge figure in baseball history for playing, creating and commerce. He created the first "Baseball Guide" and had a chain of sporting goods stores.

The Hartford Dark Blues started in 1874 and played two seasons in the National Association of Professional baseball before moving to the National League in 1876.

Their most famous fan was Samuel Clemens. "Mark Twain" was his pen name and most knew him as one of the great novelists in American history, but he was also one of the great baseball enthusiasts of his era.

Their best home run hitter was Lipman Pike, one of the Jewish pioneers of baseball.

Tom Barlow invented the bunt. The team's owner, Morgan G. Bulkeley, was the first president of the National League. Their third baseman, Bob Ferguson was their manager.

Twain's first Dark Blues game was against Boston in 1875. Spalding was on the hill for the Boston team. His squad came out on top with the 10-5 win. After that, Clemens name would show up in the Hartford Courant, who seemed to follow his every move. In his novel "A Connecticut Yankee in King Arthur's Court" (1889), he wrote about umpiring. Something he had an interest in doing but never actually followed through with.

The food industry was exploding in the United States around that time. Ballpark food took a long time to come around, but other delights were eaten before games like the Hamburger (invented in the 1880's). Hot dogs (invented in 1867) were more of a sausage and that didn't reach ballparks until the New York Giants introduced them at the Polo Grounds in 1901.

Cracker Jacks were sold around 1896 and are still a staple at most baseball games. Peanuts were in that same era. Soda rounded out the menu and that was about it.

You didn't have lobster rolls, pizza, fajitas or sushi. Fans came through the turnstiles mainly to see a ballgame. In those days eating was secondary.

Neighborhoods change, food changes, costs are skyrocketing, but the one constant through all of this is the game. You still need four balls for a walk, nine innings, three outs per inning, and no time limit. There are no periods, no break in the action, no cheerleaders and no advertising on the uniforms, not yet at least.

Even with rules changes that have occurred and others that will in the future the game endures. After all of these years hitting a small white ball being tossed between 90-100 miles per hour is still nearly impossible.

PIONEERS OF BASEBALL

JACK ROWE

JACK ROWE was a shortstop that starred for the Buffalo Bisons from 1879 to 1885. He had a 12-year career (also playing catcher and outfield) and led the National League in triples with 11 in 1881. He swiped 22 bases and reached a career-high 96 RBIs in 1887. Rowe was one of the "Big Four", which included Dan Brouthers, Hardy Richardson and Deacon White, who all played in Western New York until 1885. That year, Rowe made $2,100 (his highest salary was $3,500). The Bisons still exist in Buffalo to this day, as the AAA affiliate of the Toronto Blue Jays.

CONNIE MACK

CONNIE MACK played four seasons with the Washington Nationals before joining the Bisons of the Players' League in 1890. The light-hitting catcher invested his life savings of $500 to buy into the team and they went belly up after finishing dead last with a record of 36-96, 46 ½ games out of first place. Managed by Rowe, Mack had his best offensive season in 1890, hitting .266, with 15 doubles, 12 triples and 53 RBI and leading the league in hit by pitches with 20.*

*More about Mack on page 31.

JAY FAATZ

FAATZ, Captain, Clevelands

THE BISONS were the fourth and final stop for this first baseman, who at 6'4", 196 lb. was big for the era. Faatz was 24 when he got his big break with the Pittsburgh Alleghenys of the American Association, but was out of professional baseball for three years before re-emerging with the Cleveland Blues. After making $2,200 with the Cleveland Spiders in 1889, he signed on with Buffalo, but only played in 32 games and hit a paltry .189. His contribution was so minimal that Harper's Weekly didn't include Faatz in their 1890 Baseball Preview.

DUMMY HOY

WILLIAM "DUMMY" HOY was the first deaf player to play major league baseball (he lost his hearing after contracting meningitis as a three-year-old). The 5'6', 160 lb. centerfielder played high school ball at the Ohio School for the Deaf and broke into pro ball at age 26, playing two seasons for the Washington Nationals before joining Buffalo in 1890. Hoy accepted his ignorant nickname, but raised awareness for many others. After the Bisons folded, he played one season in the American Association and most of his 14-year career with the Cincinnati Reds. Hoy knew how to get on base, steal bases and pile up the hits each season. He was inducted into the Reds Hall of Fame in 2003, but Cooperstown is still waiting.

JOE HORNUNG

JOE HORNUNG started his career with the Bisons in 1879 as an outfielder. He hit .266 and then career-high 11 triples in his second and final season with Buffalo before moving on to the National League, where he was known for his fielding prowess. Hornung led all outfields in fielding percentage with Boston in 1881-84, 1886 and 1887. The native New Yorker was a fast runner, a base stealer, a terrific all-around ballplayer. Later in his career he managed to pull down $2,000 per season.

AL MAUL

NICKNAMED "SMILING AL", Maul pitched for six National League teams over a 15-year-career. After breaking in with the Philadelphia Keystones of the Union Association in 1884, Maul joined the Quakers in 1887. At 21, the right-hander went 4-2 with a 5.54 ERA in seven games. The Philly native was a pretty good at the plate, hitting .304 with one homerun, four RBIs and five steals and 15 walks in 56 at-bats as a first baseman and outfielder. Maul played for Pittsburgh, Washington and Brooklyn before returning to the City of Brotherly Love in 1900 to play for the Phillies. In 1888, his salary spiked to $2,800 with the Pittsburgh Alleghenys.

BEN SANDERS

SANDERS JOINED the Quakers in 1888 and he soon assumed the role of their front-line starter. The right-hander won 19 games in each of his two seasons with Philadelphia. He threw 275 innings in his first year and just over 349 in his sophomore season, ranking him seventh in the National League. Sanders led the league with eight shutouts as a rookie and lost a bid for a perfect game in the 9th inning. The Quakers also used Sanders at first base and the outfield as well. He hit .246 in 236 at-bats in 1888 and .278 in 169 at-bats the following year.

DEACON MCGUIRE

Deacon McGuire was a superb hitting and defensive catcher. In 1895, he threw out a record-breaking 189 base runners; a record that still stands. He was known for his big hands and would stuff beefsteak in the back of the catcher's glove as padding (manufacturers later used felt and hair). McGuire left his mark on the game with his record 6,856 career putouts, which stood until 1925. In 1901 an x-ray of his left hand showed 36 breaks, twists or bumps thanks to his position of 26 years. In 1901, he pulled in $3,000 with the Brooklyn Superbas.

GEORGE WOOD

Nicknamed "Dandy", George Wood played five seasons in Detroit and led the National League with 7 homeruns in 1882 before joining the Quakers in 1886. The solid-hitting left fielder hit a career-high 14 homers in 1887 for Philadelphia and drove in 66 runs. Wood is believed to be the first major leaguer from Canadian province of Prince Edward Island. He was inducted into the Canadian Baseball Hall of Fame in 2011. In 1889, his salary topped out at $2,500 with the Quakers.

THE HARTFORD DARK BLUES

SAMUEL CLEMENS

SAMUEL CLEMENS (better known to his readers as Mark Twain) made much more money than the baseball players of his era, but was a huge fan of the game and attended a lot of Dark Blues games after moving to Hartford in 1874. The Boston Globe published Twain's biting baseball musings, such as "Any ball is a strike that passes within eight feet of the plate" and "Parties who guy the umpire will be killed." In his day, baseball was the National Pastime and clearly was an obsession for him. Twain watched the Dark Blues finish in third place in their two seasons in the National League. It was reported that he even attended baseball games while spending time in Bermuda.

BOB FERGUSON

Bob Ferguson was a utility player in Hartford from 1875 to 1877 and helped lure some star players to the Dark Blues during his tenure. The third baseman never hit a home run in his time with the Dark Blues, but was a good hitter and had a knack for getting on base. In 1876, Ferguson made 54 errors in 69 games. His real claim to fame was being a switch hitter. The native New Yorker once threatened to knock out a reporter's teeth and ram his fist down a teammate's throat, but also showed a compassionate side by helping to organize a benefit game (possibly the first Old-Timers' Game) to aid a family of a young teammate who drowned while fishing.

JACK MANNING

JACK MANNING played 31 games in the outfield and first base as a 19-year-old rookie in Boston in 1873. Albert Spalding was the star pitcher of the Red Stockings that season, throwing 496 2/3 innings and going 41-14 in 60 games. Manning was a part of Boston's second consecutive National Association Championship, but was loaned to Baltimore the next season. He returned to Boston in 1875, playing in 77 games, hitting .270 with a homer and 46 RBI and also went 16-2 as a starting pitcher (Spalding was 54-5, tossing 570 ⅔ innings). They were the team's only two hurlers and won their fourth consecutive championship. Manning went 18-5 in 1876 and 1-0 as a reliever in 1878, his final season.

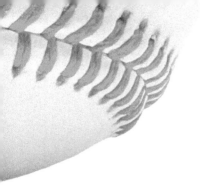

THE PHILADELPHIA PHILLIES

PHILADELPHIA CLUB 1884

IN 1884, CONSTRUCTION was completed on Philadelphia City Hall, which was the tallest building in the city for almost a century. That year, National League owners voted to have two separate player benches, since they didn't like players talking to each other during games. The Philadelphia Quakers finished sixth in the eight-team league and remarkably had 21 of their 39 wins against the Cleveland Blues and Detroit Wolverines. The first World's Championship Series took place between the Providence Grays and the New York Metropolitans, with Providence sweeping the series 3-0.

JOE MULVEY

JOE MULVEY played a total of eight years for the Phillies. The 5-11, 178 pound third baseman began his professional career as a shortstop. He made six errors in a single game (a major league record) in 1884 and used a glove literally no bigger than his hands.. Mulvey was an excellent run producer and a solid base stealer, had 28 career home runs, 532 RBI and 598 runs scored. His best season was in 1887, when Mulvey had 78 RBI and 43 steals.

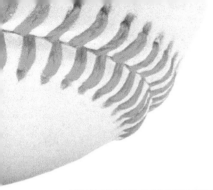

CRAVATH HOME RUN

averaged an over .400 on-base percentage twice. His 24 homers in 1915 were the record for modern day baseball and helped lead the Phillies to the World Series, but facing a Boston rotation of Rube Foster, Dutch Leonard and Ernie Shore, Philadelphia lost to the Red Sox in five games. Cravath hit an anemic .125, with no home runs and 1 RBI. A young lefty named George Herman Ruth watched the Series from the Boston bench. The future Sultan of Swat was primarily a pitcher in his rookie season and went 18-8, but Ruth did not throw an inning in the post-season and had only had one at-bat.

Gavvy Cravath hitting a home run wasn't an unusual sight if you were a Philadelphia Phillies fan in the early 1900's. In 1912, the 31-year-old outfilelder joined the Phillies. Before that, he had less than 400 big league at-bats. The Phillies struck gold, as Cravath led the National League in homers for six times, knocked in 100 RBIs and

THE PHILADELPHIA PHILLIES

THE PHILADELPHIA QUAKERS

THESE DAPPER looking gentlemen made up the 1886 Quakers squad from Philadelphia. Deacon McGuire, George Wood, Joe Mulvey, Charlie Bastian, Andy Cusick, Sid Farrar, Ed Daily, Jim Fogarty, Harry Wright (Manager), Ed Andrews, Charlie Ferguson, Arthur Irwin and Casey Clements. The team finished 71-43 and in fourth place in the National League. Wright was a former player born in Sheffield, England and is credited with coming up with the innovation of infielders backing each other up after a throw from the outfield and defensive shifts. These shifts are hugely popular today. Wright was inducted into the National Baseball Hall of Fame in 1952 by the Veterans Committee.

CHARLIE FERGUSON

CHARLIE FERGUSON was a right-handed starter who pitched with the Quakers for four years and had a 99-64 career record with a 2.67 ERA. In his rookie season, he won 21 games, but followed up with 25 losses in his sophomore campaign. In 1885, Ferguson threw a no-hitter, the following year he had a career-high 30 wins and went 22-10 in his final season. He also was an effective hitter occasionally was used at second base. Ferguson had a .288 career average, with six home runs and 157 RBI in just 257 games. He had a chance to be an all-time great, but before the 1888 season he contracted typhoid fever and passed away at the young age of 24.

CONNIE MACK

ONNIE MACK as a manager is the picture that's indelibly burned into many minds. Baseball fan or not, we've heard of "Connie Mack Leagues" that are in virtually every town in America. That came because of a 'code of conduct' that he created after the 1916 season. Mack's legend started to grow in 1901 when he became the manager, treasurer and part-owner of the Philadelphia Athletics. He remained in the dugout through the 1950 season and retired at the age of 87 with astounding record was 3582-3814, nine American League pennants, eight World Series appearances and five Championships(1910-11, 1913, 1929-30). A true Hall of Famer and baseball legend.

MUTUALS OF NEW YORK TEAM PICTURE

the season when they refused to play on the West Coast due to financial restrictions. The Mutuals were replaced as tenants at the Union Grounds by a team called "Hartford of Brooklyn", possibly the most confusing name in the history of professional baseball.

THE MUTUALS of New York first played at Elysian Fields in Hoboken, NJ and later moved to Union Grounds in Brooklyn in 1868. In 1871, they became a charter member in the first professional league. In 1872, the Mutuals were third in the league in attendance drawing 40,500 spectators. In 1876, they joined the National League and made their mark in the record books with the first-ever triple play against the Hartford Dark Blues, but were expelled from the league after

JOE START

Nicknamed "Old Reliable", Joe Start began his career during the American Civil War. In 1871, Start joined the Mutuals (who played in the National Association) at 28 years old and started to make an impact as his playing time increased. In 1876, he continued with the Mutuals as they entered the National League. The steady first baseman played six seasons in New York, followed by brief stops in Hartford and Chicago, before a seven-year stint with Providence where he won a World Championship in 1884. Start only had one hit in 10 post-season at-bats, but did manage an RBI. He finished his career with the Washington Nationals in 1886, at the age of 43. He earned $1,300 towards the end of his career.

PECK AND SNYDER CARD

SCORECARD

THIS PECK AND SNYDER card looks to be portraying a player from 1869 Cincinnati Red Stockings. The Sporting Goods Company was located not too far from Wall Street in New York City. They also produced team photo cards for the New York Mutuals, Chicago White Stockings and Philadelphia Athletics. Andrew Peck and Irving Snyder made these promotional cards, which have turned into very rare collectibles and possibly the first baseball cards in existence. In 1875, they offered baseball caps in their catalog. Baseball was the top sport in the United States and this company wanted to cash in on that. Albert Spalding eventually purchased the business when they expanded.

JOHN CLAPP

JOHN CLAPP was nicknamed "Honest John" and joined the Athletics in 1873 after one year with the Middletown Mansfields. His nickname is derived from an incident during his career when a bookie offered $5,000 to allow a passed ball with runners on base. Clapp asked when he should do that so he could place the bet and then promptly alerted the authorities. The versatile ballplayer played catcher and outfield and had three decent seasons with the Athletics, hitting .304 and .291 in his first two seasons. During his last season is when he became a player-manager for the New York Gothams.

NAPOLEON LAJOIE

establishing an American League single-season record .426 average. Some called Lajoie the best second baseman in history, retiring with 3,420 hits. His 2,521 hits at the end of his career were an American League record, until Ty Cobb surpassed that mark. Lajoie was inducted in the second class of the National Baseball Hall of Fame in 1937.

NAPOLEON LAJOIE was one of the greats to ever grace the diamond in the City of Brotherly Love. Nicknamed "The Frenchman", he signed with the Phillies in 1896 after the team purchased him and another player for $1,500. Lajoie averaged .345 in his five National League seasons before jumping to the Athletics in 1901 and

CHARLES BASTIAN AND DENNY LYONS

1888. In 1885, the light hitting infielder led the league in strikeouts with 82, a very high number for the era. His claim to fame is he played for the Union League, National League, Players' League and American Association. In 1886 he was paid $1,600 by the Quakers.

THIS ACTION SHOT of Quakers second baseman Charlie Bastian trying to tag out Providence third baseman Denny Lyons shows off what baseball was like back in the late 19th Century. The Philadelphia-born Bastian played all around the diamond (mostly shortstop and also played second and third base) from 1885-

ATHLETICS BBC TEAM SHOT. BROOKLYN -PHILADELPHIA CHAMPIONSHIP GAME 1866

THE CHAMPIONSHIP GAME between the Philadelphia Athletics and Atlantic of Brooklyn was featured in Harper's Weekly in 1866. Somehow the champion team from Brooklyn split the two-game series with the Athletics and retained their championship. 8,000 tickets were sold for the post-season rate of 25 cents (tickets during the regular season were 10 cents). Scorecards were handed out, which may have been the first time the public could keep score. Somewhere between 22,000 and 32,000 showed up for the first game in Philadelphia, but it was postponed because of a fight between a fan and the police in the bottom of the first inning. The game moved to Brooklyn on October 15th, 14 days later. Brooklyn won Game 1, 27-17. The series went back to Philadelphia on October 22nd, where the police were in force and a fence had been built. The Athletics won the game 31-12 after the game had been called due to rain in the top of the eighth inning. They never scheduled a third game.

OLIVER TEBEAU

OLIVER WENDELL "PATSY" TEBEAU played third base for the Chicago White Stockings, His career in Chicago began in 1887, but he only got into 20 games, registering only 10 RBI's and swiping eight bases. He went on to play 12 more seasons, mainly with the Cleveland Spiders. He did some player/managing for Cleveland in the Players' League, the Spiders, St, Louis Perfectos and St. Louis Cardinals. With the Cardinals, third baseman John J. McGraw may have been the real manager while Tebeau seemed to be a "face" but not the brains. Apparently, his claim to fame was abusing umpires and the opposition. The press didn't like it and chronicled most of it. Post-baseball, he ran a saloon in St. Louis. After his wife left him in 1918, he took his own life by shooting himself in the head. Suicide was a common fate of many players from the Deadball era.

JAMES EDWARD O'NEILL

JAMES EDWARD O'NEILL was nicknamed "Tip" and the "Woodstock Wonder" due to his birthplace being Woodstock, Ontario. O'Neill started as a pitcher but became an everyday leftfielder for the St. Louis Browns (renamed the Cardinals in 1900) for seven of his ten years in professional baseball. At 6'1", he had power and was a run producer. In 1886, he led the Cardinals to a World Championship over Chicago, hitting .400 and slugging two home runs. He twice led the American Association with 107 and 123 runs batted in. His career year was in 1887, when he won the Triple Crown (second person in baseball to achieve that feat) with a .435 average (second highest average in the record books), led the league with 167 runs, 225 hits, 52 doubles, 19 triples and 14 home runs. It's one of the greatest years in professional baseball and that solidified him in St. Louis. He's in the Canadian Baseball Hall of Fame and has been dubbed the "Canadian" Babe Ruth. He made $2,600 in 1889 with the Brown Stockings.

WILLIAM BUCK EWING

WILLIAM "BUCK" EWING was possibly the best catcher of his era and one of the greats in the history of the game. The first three years of his Hall of Fame career were spent with the Troy Trojans of the National League, where he caught, played shortstop and the outfield. Ewing hit only two home runs in three seasons with the Trojans, but slugged 10 home runs, hit .303 and scored 90 runs for the New York Gothams in 1883 and 20 triples in 1884. That was the beginning of an exceptional stretch in his 18-year career, that saw him hit .303, with and 883 runs batted in and 354 steals. Technically he has the record as a catcher, but it's not considered the modern-day record under the new rules. Ewing made $5,500 with the New York Giants in 1891.

HARRY McCORMICK

HARRY McCORMICK pitched and played right field for just four seasons in professional baseball. Patrick Henry was his given name and he broke in with the Syracuse Stars in 1879 at the age of 23. In his first and only season there, McCormick was 18-33 with 49 complete games. The Stars went 22-48, so his 18 wins were just four less than the entire team that season. At the plate, he hit .222 with one home run and 21 RBIs. His only home run proved to be historic, as it was the only run in a game the Stars would win 1-0. A pitcher hitting a homer for the only run has never been duplicated in Major League Baseball since. The team folded on September 10, 1879 without finishing their one National League season.

RED STOCKINGS TEAM PHOTO

THE CINCINNATI Red Stockings were founded in 1869 and were baseball's first professional team. Harry Wright owned them and paid 10 players from March 15th to November 15th. Cincinnati went 65-0 in 1869, the only undefeated season in the history of professional baseball. Some would say they paid the right players. They were also the first team to play on the East and West coasts in the same season. The Red Stockings are credited with growing the sport in its early days. On June 14, 1870, Cincinnati lost 8-7 to the Brooklyn Atlantics in front of an impressive 20,000 fans in New York, ending an unbelievable 84-game winning streak. This team is loosely connected to today's Cincinnati Reds.

CHARLIE GOULD

CHARLIE GOULD played six years of professional baseball, the last two (1886-87) with the Reds. The six-footer was a light hitting, but good fielding first baseman and earned the nickname "The Bushel Basket". His errant throw in the 11th inning ended the Red Stockings 84-game winning streak in 1870. Gould was a good guy in the clubhouse. After he retired, he became a police officer in the Cincinnati area. He was a captain in New Haven in 1875 and gets credited for managing those games.

BASEBALL IN LOUISVILLE

THE LOUISVILLE COLONELS had an interesting history. They were in the American Association from 1882-1891. From 1882-1884, they were known as the Louisville Eclipse. In 1884, pitcher Guy Hecker started 75 games and led the league in wins (52), strikeouts (385) and earned run average (1.80), winning the Triple Crown of pitching.

His team went 68-40 and came in third place. In 1892, the Colonels moved to the National League when the American Association ceased to exist. Honus Wagner made his debut in Eclipse Stadium as a member of the Colonels in 1897. The Hall of Famer played there until 1899. A fire in the grandstand forced the team to finish out the season on the road. Owner Barney Dreyfuss sold his interest in the team to gain controlling interest of the Pittsburgh Pirates in 1900 and took Wagner and 13 Colonels players with him. The high water mark was 1890, when the Colonels won the pennant and tied the National League champion Brooklyn Bridegrooms (later known as the Dodgers) in the World Series 3-3 with one tie. No champion was crowned.

BALTIMORE BASEBALL CLUB 1894

1894 WAS A GOOD YEAR for Baseball in Baltimore. The Orioles won their first National League Pennant in convincing fashion. They won 24 of the last 25 games to end the regular season. From 1894-1897, the winner of the best-of-seven series won the Temple Cup. The Orioles played the second place New York Giants and were swept. Two of the six future Hall of Fame players involved in the series were John McGraw and Wee Willie Keeler. The Giants had future Hall of Fame pitcher Amos Rusie, and star outfielder George Van Haltren. Baltimore bounced back to win the Cup in 1896 and1897. From 1882-1891, the Orioles were in the American Association and moved to the NL in 1892. After the 1899 season, the NL reduced from 12 teams to 8 and they were out.

MIKE LEHANE

MIKE LEHANE played for the Columbus Solons for two seasons. He was a consistent and solid first baseman who played 277 games in the American Association. He broke in as a 25-year-old in 1890 and led the league in games played (140) and had 56 RBI and 13 steals to help his team finish in second place. Lehane put up almost identical numbers in his second season and led the league in fielding percentage, assists and double plays turned by a first baseman. He was a pipe fitter by trade in his hometown of New York City and died in 1903 from chronic kidney nephritis or an autoimmune disease.

NEW GROUNDS OF METROPOLITAN BASEBALL CLUB IN STATEN ISLAND

a stocky fellow who hit 31 triples in 1886 (a record that stood for 25 years). When the season ended, the team folded. Orr was sold to the Brooklyn Bridegrooms along with seven other players that October.

THE NEW YORK METROPOLITANS of the American Association played at the St. George Cricket Grounds for two seasons. In 1886, they were 53-82 and finished in seventh place. In 1887, they went 44-89 and once again finished seventh. First baseman Dave Orr was a standout, hitting .368 with 66 RBI. At 5'11", 180 lbs, Orr was

BOSTON BEANEATERS

EZRA SUTTON

Ezra Sutton was a utility player who played a dozen of his 18 seasons with the Boston Redcaps/ Beaneaters of the National League. Sutton .346 and led the league with 162 hits in 1884. Twice in his career, Sutton led the league in double plays for third baseman. After the NL was formed in 1876, he was one of the first players to collect 1,000 career hits. He ended his career with 1,574 hits and three pennants with Boston (1877, 1878, 1883).

BOSTON BEANEATERS

JOHN MORRILL

JOHN MORRILL had a 13-year career with Boston Beaneaters from 1876-1888. He played six positions and was a run producer who hit for power. He had 33 doubles, 16 triples and six home runs with 68 RBI and led Boston to a pennant in 1883 after taking over the managerial job in the middle of the season. In 1887, he achieved career-highs in home runs (12), RBI's (81) and hits (141), along with his 32 doubles in 127 games and led the National League. He also won the pennant in 1877, 1878 and 1883 with the Beaneaters. "Honest John" finished out his career in Boston with the Reds in the Players' League in 1890. They won the championship that season. He was one of the last bare-handed catchers.

TOMMY McCARTHY

Tommy McCarthy was a star outfielder for the St. Louis Browns and later with the Boston Beaneaters. In 1893, he had 111 RBI's and then topped that with 126 the following year, along with 13 home runs (second in the league to teammate Hugh Duffy). The duo were called the "Heavenly Twins". McCarthy had a .292 career average, could drive in runs and finished his career with 468 steals. The Veteran's Committee voted him into the Baseball Hall of Fame in 1946.

DETROIT WOLVERINES

DETROIT BASEBALL CLUB 1887

named after star catcher Charlie Bennett, who tragically lost both of his legs in a train accident that ended his fine career. That name lasted until 1912. The team folded following the 1888 season because of financial constraints. They were the first professional team in the history of the Motor City to win a championship.

THE DETROIT WOLVERINES were members of the National League from 1881-1888 and had 1,286 fans in the stands for their first game. The team won the pennant in 1887, beating the American Association champions St. Louis Browns 10 games to five to capture the World Championship. Sam Thompson was the hitting star for Detroit with a .362 average. The Wolverines played in rickety old Recreation Park, which had to be demolished in 1894. The club moved into Bennett Park in 1896 on the corner of Michigan and Trumball, it was

TOMMY BOND

Tommy Bond was a notable pitcher and right fielder for the Boston Red Stockings of the National League. He hailed from Granard, Ireland and was the first major league baseball player born in "The Emerald Isle" to play in the big leagues. In 1874, Bond won 22 games with the Brooklyn Atlantics and won 50 games the next two seasons with Hartford. In 1877, he won baseball's first Triple Crown of pitching (wins, earned run average and strikeouts) and put up back-to-back 40 win seasons in 1878 and 1879. Although he played some outfield, Bond made his mark as a pitcher, the right-hander ended his 10-year career with a stellar 234-163 record, 2.14 ERA and threw over 500 innings three times. In 1880, he made $1,500 with the Red Stockings.

NED HANLON

NICKNAMED "FOXY NED", Hanlon was known as the "Father of Modern Day Baseball". His playing career included 30 career home runs, 517 RBI and 329 steals, plus an 1887 pennant with the Detroit Wolverines. With Baltimore, Hanlon got credited for inventing the "inside baseball" strategy. He utilized the hit and run, the squeeze play, the sacrifice bunt (something some fans hate in today's game), the double steal and the "Baltimore Chop"; which is when a player intentionally hit the ball in the dirt as hard as they could in front of home plate to cause a high bouncer that was difficult to field and throw out a runner. As a manager in Baltimore, Hanlon helped to build a winning team. It took a number of years for the Baseball Hall of Fame to induct managers and Hanlon got in well after his death in 1996 via the Veterans Committee. In 1889, he made a cool $3,100 with the Pittsburgh Alleghenys as a player.

DAN BROUTHERS

"**B**IG DAN" BROUTHERS was a 6'2", 207 lb. first baseman, a giant of his sport at the time and a major power hitter from 1879-1896. His career slugging percentage of .519 was at the time a major-league record (with at least 4,000 at-bats) until Ty Cobb broke it in 1922. The amazing part about being the premier power hitter of the dead ball era was that the best home run total was eight with Buffalo in 1881. Brouthers hit double-digits three times with a high of 14. He drove in 100 or more runs five times, with a career-high of 124 with the Brooklyn Grooms in 1892. He retired with four batting titles, a career .342 average, 460 doubles, 205 triples, 1,296 RBI and 256 steals. He was one of only 29 players in the history of the game to appear in four decades and was voted into the Hall of Fame in 1945 by the Veterans Committee. He won a championship in Detroit in 1887 and an NL Pennant in Baltimore in 1894.

KANSAS CITY COWBOYS

KANSAS CITY COWBOYS 1888.

KANSAS CITY COWBOYS is clearly one of the first cool names for a sports franchise. Their first season was in 1888 and they went 43-89 in the American Association. The Cowboys played at Association Park and moved to Exposition Park in 1889, where they played college football and minor league baseball as well. Bill Fagan was a one-year veteran who pitched and played outfield that inaugural season. He was 5-11 as a pitcher and hit .215 with three doubles. Another pitcher, Henry Porter won 18 games and lost 37.

In 1889, their win total increased to 55 games and they moved up from eighth to seventh place, but still finished 27 games under .500. Outfielder Jim Burns and Billy Hamilton were standouts. Burns knocked in 97 RBIs and hit .304, while Hamilton stole 111 bases. Hamilton hit .403 after he left Kansas City and is third all-time in steals . He was voted in the Hall of Fame in 1961 via the Veterans Committee. This franchise folded after the 1889 season.

GEORGE FISHER

GEORGE FISHER was busy in 1884. He played for both the Cleveland Blues in the National League and his hometown Wilmington Quicksteps in the American Association. He played 14 games at 5 different positions and hit .094 for the pair of squads. The Quicksteps were a late season replacement team after the Philadelphia Keystones folded due to lack of attendance and went 2-16 (12th in the league).

ED ANDREWS (QUAKERS) SAM BARKLEY (TOLEDO)

IN 1884, BARKLEY broke into baseball at the age of 26 with Toledo. Andrews played for the Philadelphia Quakers. Both played second base, but were versatile and played other positions. Both were good players, so what's the connection? At some point, both players paths crossed. They're practically wearing the same suits, so they took this picture together to show off their awesomeness. It looks like the picture was taken in Toledo, so Barkley gets credit for setting up this shot.

CHICAGO WHITE SOX

CHARLIE SPRAGUE

CHARLIE SPRAGUE was a pitcher and outfielder for the Chicago White Sox in 1887, when they were in the National League. This shows him on the pitcher's mound, with maybe a bag of rosin by his side? At the age of 22, Sprague broke in with the Sox, but he only pitched in three games. After a year away from the game, Sprague returned to play in the American Association for the Cleveland Spiders (1889) and the Toledo Maumees (1890), where he went 9-5. His career numbers are 10-7.

BASEBALL CARD MANUFACTURER

IRVING SNYDER

Iʀᴠɪɴɢ Sɴʏᴅᴇʀ started the Peck and Snyder Sporting Goods company in 1866. They were in Manhattan and like most successful businesses they advertised. In 1870, they produced team cards and that may have been the very start of the baseball card craze.

REN MULFORD

Ren Mulford was a reporter for the Sporting Life, a 19th century national newspaper and magazine and wrote for them from 1888 to 1917, when they ceased operations. Mulford hailed from Cincinnati, Ohio and was the sports editor for the Cincinnati Post and worked for the Cincinnati Enquirer. He popularized the word "fan" (which is short for fanatic). He never wanted to take credit for that and would give it to another writer of his day.

HENRY CHADWICK

Henry Chadwick wrote about the development of the game and was known as the "Father of Baseball", which is unusual since he was born in England. He edited the first baseball guide that was sold to the public and created the box score, which a perfect way to encapsulate what happened in a game that fans could follow, even if they didn't watch the game. Chadwick is credited with creating earned run average and batting average. He also thought of the "K" on the scorecard to denote a strikeout. He accomplished so much and was inducted into the National Baseball Hall of Fame in 1938 well after his death.

CAL McVEY

CAL MCVEY was a ladies man, who happened to be very good at the game of baseball. He was described as "powerful and barrel chested" in the newspapers and was a big part of a Boston Red Stockings team that Harry Wright put together for their first championship in 1872. McVey caught for the first two seasons and then moved to the outfield. He led the National Association in hits and runs batted in twice. After leaving Boston, he joined Chicago of the National League and set a record for recording two consecutive six-hit games in 1876.

TOMMY BEALS

Tommy Beals first broke into professional baseball with the Washington Olympics in 1871 under the alias W. Thomas. When that team went belly up just nine games into the 1872 season, he joined the Toledo Blue Stockings. In 1874, he joined the Boston Braves and was part of the Red Stockings first place clubs in 1874 and 1875. The 5'5", 144 lb. Beals was an adequately sized second baseman, but a bit on the small side for a catcher. He did have a flair for fashion, wearing white shoes which were very uncommon for the era.

JOE BATTIN

JOE BATTIN was born and raised in Philadelphia and had a chance to play for his hometown Athletics for two years (1873-74) of his ten-year career. He hit .300 for the St. Louis Brown Stockings in 1877, but also led the 300 once, but also made 57 errors at second and third base that season. In 1936, Battin made the ballot for induction to the National Baseball Hall of Fame. He got only one vote.

PROVIDENCE BASEBALL CLUB, 1879.

THE PROVIDENCE Baseball Club of 1879 were better known as the Providence Grays, who were in existence until 1885. In January 1878, Henry Root was hired as the team president and Benjamin Douglas was hired as the team's general manager. Just over a year later, Root fired Douglas for incompetence and insubordination. In 1879, the Grays finished first with a 59-25 record. The star of the team was John Montgomery Ward. He went on to have a celebrated 17-year career as a pitcher and a hitter. He was 47-19 in 1879 and he threw 587 innings.

HARRY BUCKNER

HARRY BUCKNER pitched, played catcher, infield and outfield for the Royal Giants of Brooklyn, one of the best squads in the Negro Leagues. Black players played in this league or they didn't play at all in the United States. In 1909, at the age of 33, Buckner was still pitching nine-inning gems. Later in his career, he played baseball in Cuba, one of the few Americans who played there. Sportswriter Harry Daniels named him to his 1909 "All-American team". He played with the Giants for one more season and played 23 seasons in all.

J.W. CONNORS (OWNER)

J.W. CONNORS was the owner and manager of the Royal Giants of Brooklyn baseball club, which he formed in 1905. They were a barnstorming club who played against white semi-pro teams to start. Some of their stars included Smokey Joe Williams and John Henry "Pop" Lloyd. New York Yankees legends Babe Ruth and Lou Gehrig played against the Giants on these barnstorming tours. The team disbanded in 1942. He was also the owner of Brooklyn Royal Cafe.

GEORGE PINKNEY 1888

GEORGE PINKNEY was a third baseman who broke in with the Cleveland Blues in 1884 and played for Brooklyn from 1886-1891. He helped the Brooklyn Bridegrooms win an American Association Pennant in 1889 and National League pennant in 1890. The franchise later turned into the Brooklyn Dodgers. Pinkney hit a career high of .309 in 1890 and stole 296 bases in his career. When he retired, he had the iron man record of 577 consecutive games in his career. His record of 5,152 consecutive innings held for the last 95 years until Cal Ripken Jr. broke it in 1985.

TOMMY CORCORAN

TOMMY CORCORAN was a shortstop who played in Brooklyn from 1892-1896. In 1894, he scored 123 runs, hit .300 and 92 RBIs. Early in his career, he fielded without a glove. Later, Corcoran set a major-league record (that still stands) with 14 assists at shortstop in a nine-inning game. He played for 18 years and then became an umpire for one season in the failed Federal League. He had 2,256 career hits, along with 1,135 RBI and 387 stolen bases. In 1904, he pulled down $3,300 with the Cincinnati Reds.

BROOKLYN ATLANTICS

ATLANTICS OF BROOKLYN, 1869

THE BROOKLYN ATLANTICS of 1869 were already a team rich with championships and one of the first to call themselves a professional team. In 1859, they were the champions of the National Association of Base Ball Players with an 11-1 record. They held that title through the 1861 season, which was shortened due to the outbreak of the Civil War. They won eight pennants in total, including 1869. The Atlantics played in the Capitoline Grounds from 1864-1872 and the Union Grounds from 1873-1875.

BROOKLYN ATLANTICS

PETER O'BRIEN

Peter O'Brien played for the Brooklyn Atlantics from 1856 to 1865. His brother Matty played for the team as well. Matty was a pitcher and Peter played shortstop. Both brothers also played cricket on a part-time basis. They played in front of crowds that could reach 15,000. He was one of the players who helped shape the sport in the early days. Peter also became the team treasurer in 1856.

EXCELSIOR'S OF BROOKLYN, 1869

THE EXCELSIOR'S OF BROOKLYN played in some memorable games. They were formed in 1854. Some of their big stars were pitchers Jim Creighton, Asa Brainard and Candy Cummings (who is credited with inventing the curveball). In 1860, the Excelsior's started to wear the ancestor to the modern-day baseball cap. They were almost the National Association champions in 1860. In Game 3 against the Brooklyn Atlantics, the game had to be called due to a rowdy crowd. It was a tie, but Brooklyn was recognized as the true champions. The Excelsior's once toured around New York, playing in various cities.

ELMER FOSTER

ELMER FOSTER played from 1886 to 1891 mostly as an outfielder. He started with the New York Metropolitans and then played the next two seasons with the New York Giants of the National League. In 1888, Foster had 10 RBI and stole 13 bases. In 1889, he only played in two games. Both seasons, the Giants finished in first place and won the World Championship. In 1888, they beat the St. Louis Browns and bested the Brooklyn Bridegrooms (American Association champions) in 1889.

REFERENCES FOR PIONEERS OF BASEBALL

WIKIPEDIA

http://www.twainquotes.com/TwainBaseball.html

http://www.history.com/news/the-history-of-ballpark-food

http://www.crawfishboxes.com/2013/7/18/4534850/on-hot-dogs-peanuts-cracker-jack-the-history-of-ballpark-food

rootsandroutes.net

WIKICOMMONS

www.baseball-reference.com

www.baseball-almanac.com

Sabr - Society of Baseball Research

NATIONAL BASEBALL HALL OF FAME

dummyhoy.com

retrosheet.org

Morris, Peter. Baseball Fever: Early Baseball in Michigan. Ann Arbor: University of Michigan Press, 2003.

A Game of Inches: The Stories Behind the Innovations That Shaped Baseball, The Game on the Field. Chicago: Ivan R. Dee, 2006.

http://www.smithsonianmag.com/arts-culture/the-invention-of-the-baseball-mitt-12799848/?-no-ist

http://sabr.org/gamesproj/game/october-1866-return-their-investment

http://www.sportscollectorsdaily.com/peck-and-snyder-the-company/ Rich Mueller article

http://www.motorcitysportsjournal.com/1887-detroit-wolverines-first-champs

http://www.findagrave.com/cgi-bin/fg.cgi?page=gr&GRid=4589

http://www.covehurst.net/ddyte/brooklyn/negro_leagues.html

http://www.seamheads.com/NegroLgs/team.php?yearID=1908.5&teamID=BRG&LGOrd=2

http://coe.k-state.edu/annex/nlbemuseum/history/players/buckner.html

http://sabr.org/gamesproj/game/august-23-1860-no-gentlemens-game-excelsior-vs-atlantic Craig B. Waff

The Irish and the Making of American Sport, 1835-1920, Patrick R. Redmond

https://sabr.org/gamesproj/game/october-1866-return-their-investment

This essay was originally published in "Inventing Baseball: The 100 Greatest Games of the 19th Century" (2013), edited by Bill Felber.

PICTURES

PICTURE CREDITS

Rowe – NYPL (use From The New York Public Library Digital Collections tag each time)

Mack - Wikipedia

Faatz - Wikipedia

Hoy – Wikipedia

Sanders – NYPL

Deacon McGuire – NYPL

George Wood – NYPL

Clemens – Wikipedia

Ferguson – Wikipedia

Manning – NYPL

1884 Phillies – NYPL

Mulvey – NYPL

Cravath – NYPL

1886 Quakers – NYPL

Connie Mack Athletics - NYPL

Mutuals of New York – NYPL

Joe Start - NYPL

Peck and Snyder – NYPL

Napoleon Lajoie – NYPL

Charles Bastian and Denny Lyons – NYPL

1866 Championship game - SABR. ORG

Oliver Tebeau – NYPL

James Edward O'Neill – NYPL

William Buck Ewing – NYPL

Harry McCormick – NYPL

Red Stockings Team Photo – NYPL

Charlie Gould – NYPL

Baseball in Louisville – Image number ULPA P_01043, R. G. Potter Collection, Photographic Archives, University of Louisville, Louisville, Kentucky.

Baltimore Baseball Club – Wikipedia

Mike Lehane – Wikipedia

Metropolitan Baseball – NYPL (Not AG Spaulding collection)

Ezra Sutton –NYPL

John Morrill – NYPLTommy McCarthy - NYPL

Detroit Baseball – NYPL

Tommy Bond – NYPL

Dan Brouthers – NYPL

KC Cowboys – NYPL

George Fisher – Wikipedia

Andrew-Barkley – NYPL

Charlie Sprague – NYPL

Irving Snyder – NYPL

Ren Mulford – NYPL

Henry Chadwick – NYPL - "The Pageant of America" Collection

Cal McVey- NYPL

Tommy Beals – NYPL

Joe Battin – NYPL

Providence Baseball Club – NYPL

Harry Buckner – NYPL

J.W. Connors – NYPL

George Pinkney – NYPL

Tommy Corcoran – NYPL

Atlantics of Brooklyn - 1869 – NYPL

Peter O'Brien – NYPL

Excelsior's of Brooklyn – NYPL

Elmer Foster – NYPL

CPSIA information can be obtained
at www.ICGtesting.com
Printed in the USA
LVOW05*0920221217
R13060800001B/R130608PG559443LVX2B/1/P

9 781628 654462